TANGLED TONGUES

TANGLED TONGUES

David Kerr

Introduction by Jack Mapanje

in association with
THE WORDSWORTH TRUST

Acknowledgements

Some of these poems have previously appeared
in the following magazines and anthologies:
*Airings, Allusions, Ariel, Carapace, Envoi,
East London Arts Magazine, The Haunting Wind,
Illuminations, Kotaz, Kunapipi, London Magazine,
Mau, Mokwadi, New Coin, Ngoma, Odi, Outlook,
Poetry as a Foreign Language, Raw Edge, Red Lamp,
Smith's Knoll, Southern African Review of Books,
Stand* and *Tantrum.*

First published in the UK in 2003 by Flambard Press
Stable Cottage, East Fourstones, Hexham NE47 5DX
in association with The Wordsworth Trust, Grasmere

Typeset by Stephen Hebron
Cover design by Gainford Design Associates
Printed in the UK by Cromwell Press, Trowbridge

A CIP catalogue record for this book
is available from the British Library.

ISBN 1 873226 60 8

© David Kerr 2003
Introduction © Jack Mapanje 2003

All rights reserved

Flambard Press wishes to thank Northern Arts
for its financial support.

website: www.flambardpress.co.uk

Contents

Introduction   7

Memory on Request	9
Virgin Express – Unscheduled Stop	10
Village	11
The Death of Frogs	12
Baobabs	12
After Worship	13
Cracked	13
Making an Impression	14
Safari Slides	15
Afro-canned	16
Gaborone	17
Floor Show	18
Swimming Pool Sacrament	20
Close Shaves	21
Elemental	22
Haunted	23
A Hard Rain	24
Programmed	25
Examinations	26
Sages	27
Starlight	28
Southern Cross	28
Tangles	29
Return of the Linguist	30
Tongues	30
Other Languages	31
Prayer Rock	32

Furnace	34
Lifestyles	37
Globalisation	37
IMF Consultant	38
A Ballad for the 'Goodies'	39
The Maxi's Last Jaunt	40
Children at Play (Leeds/Harare)	42
Kite	42
Bouquets	43
Song of the Seed Disposers	44
Seed Music	45
AIDS Ward	46
Bare Truths	47
The Continuing Search	47
Sunday Exercise	48
A Mother's Last Song	49
Working Women	50
After Chikumbi: Blood Donation	52
Tisa's War	53
Freedom Percussion	54
The Cross Examination of Sofia Nkosana	55
Uprooted	56
Our Year of Living Dangerously	58
Safe as Houses	59
High Density Housing Scheme	60
Midair Encounter	61
Other People's Houses	62
A Tongue's Biography	63
Notes	64

Introduction

When I proposed seeing the street where David Kerr was born in Carlisle, he shrugged his shoulders and wondered whether it would be worth it. We went anyway, leaving the trees, hedgerows and mountain tops of wintry Grasmere clad in snow. I wanted to see this border town not only because David was my university teacher and close friend but also because he is a human rights activist who contributed to my release from political detention in Malawi. I have always loved borders and peripheries because they so often seem to produce generous hearts. As I drove to Carlisle, childhood memories animated my friend; he pointed out the mountains he climbed, lakes rowed across, streets walked along, on the various return journeys he made to Cumbria during his many years of wandering. I was impressed by the sharp memory of the poet in the academic.

For myself, born beside Lake Malawi, which forms a natural border with Mozambique, in a tropical landscape full of rivers and mountains and the mysterious folklore surrounding them, there was something peculiarly nostalgic about the journey. It symbolised the symmetrical journeys we had made crossing continents in opposite directions. I had never travelled in the English Lake District before. But now one of the links in our friendship lay before us clad in a strange beauty. I remembered the classes in Romantic verse which David had taught me many years earlier at the University of Malawi; I was beginning to see the relevance of the Wordsworth and Coleridge poems that I'd read.

David told me he left Carlisle at a young age and lived, for purposes of education or work, in various parts of England: Blackpool, Newcastle, Coventry and London. For many years after that he only came to Cumbria on family holidays from teaching positions in Southern Africa: Zambia, Botswana and particularly Malawi, the home of his wife, Nyandovi. Now he makes regular visits to Cumbria with his grown-up children, especially since the ashes of his parents are scattered in the mountains they loved.

It is in Southern Africa that David Kerr has made his reputation as a distinguished academic and a specialist in the theatre and media of social transformation. He has achieved a rare combination of theory and practice. His academic book, *African Popular Theatre*, is a standard textbook in parts of Africa and is considered a seminal publication. At the same time he has had vast practical experience of community mobilisation through the travelling theatres, videos, radio programmes and television plays that he has been involved with over the years. This might explain why several poems in *Tangled Tongues* use dramatic monologue or other devices close to theatre.

In addition, wherever he has taught, David Kerr has been a pioneer of creative writing projects; he has been engaged in creative writing courses, writers' groups and editorial work. I have known him as a published author too. His short stories, poems, a novel and plays have been in imprints or journals throughout Southern Africa. This collection is, therefore, critical because it gives the British readership access to his poetic mind. *Tangled Tongues* provides an unusual perspective of a life shifting from one culture to another, with a persona constantly aware of the tragi-comic contradictions and ironies that such a life throws up.

The poems in this selection reflect a rich variety of themes and forms, ranging from the conventional sonnet, ballad and haiku to experimental poems, which derive to some extent from African traditions of orality. What I find most compelling about this selection is that the poet is not afraid to tackle topics which more timid British poets might veer away from but which he makes seem familiar. My visit to Carlisle on that winter morning was worthwhile, because it made me realise the enormous distance David Kerr has had to travel culturally as well as geographically. It has broadened my interpretation of the poems, and made me understand how tongues are becoming tangled everywhere in the 'globe's remotest gullies'.

Jack Mapanje, August 2002
Dove Cottage, Grasmere

Memory on Request

You wanted a poem about
that blackout, border-town,
two-up, two-down, terraced
house where I was born,
and where, as sirens wailed,
mother fixed boggle-eyed
gas masks, humouring me
with games of 'let's hide
under the table and I'll
save you from the bombs',
or how I crapped in an outside
lav, guided by Dad's
torch with beam unfurled
from shaking fingers, and how
that haven's loss hurled
me careening from fried-
bacon landlady or seedy joint
to rented bungalows around
the world. But you know
too well, such across-
the-years nostalgia needs
another safe Ithaca to sing
from, whose harbour lights
bobbing palely at prow's point
I cannot yet identify.

Virgin Express – Unscheduled Stop

The train whimpers
shuddering ... dead.
As the power is lost
and, one by one, lights
dim, we gaze through
scratched windows
at stars drilling frost
onto hills. Buttoned
against the chill,
we shuffle, refugees,
led to the buffet car
for illumination and free
crisps, pringles, cokes.
Our noses itch as
blocked lavs seep.
The tannoy crackles
a storm of speculation
or apologies, drowned
by jeers and jokes.
Strangers, entranced,
swap intimacies.
A busker establishes
his pre-Christmas pitch,
blowing a sax with
tuneless enthusiasm.
So why, beyond any
need to keep warm,
do we, like dervishes,
dance and dance?

Village

Banana leaf fronds
shimmer over lusty
twitching goats

Women in pyramids
wrinkle their noses
from wind dust

Each new arrival
kneels and bends
from the waist

claps respectful hands
and knees tucked, settles
to shell peas

deftly twist maize
from cobs or suckle
mealie fat babies

Men on dried hills
duck under cow-
kicked sandstorms

I ease an alien body
into the slow
choreography.

The Death of Frogs

In the dry season
the death of frogs
is most spectacular.

If I were a frog
would I simply stretch
belly-up like *biltong*
blackening in the sun?

Or would I shrivel
crouching, legs tensed,
on the point of leaping
to imaginary pools?

Baobabs

The baobab fruit deceives; its soft fur
hides a shell only sharp stones can blast.

Some emaciated arms may scarcely make the blows.

Inside, the acrid sherbet seeds fizz on the tongue
leaving black kernels saliva-glinting like tourmalines.

For some hollow eyes that aesthetic is their last.

After Worship

Solomon trudged in his suit for miles
each Sabbath down moss-slick paths to chant
in the valley chapel.

I would drag my white, stripped limbs
up the peak, to let boulder and blossom
sing in my blood.

On my descent I'd meet him, Bible clutched
tight, sweating upwards, and we'd exchange
sly, ecumenical smiles.

Cracked

The woman is squatting naked in the kerb
on a cushion of striped asylum-issue rags.
Youths giggle and kick dust; unperturbed,
she claps a pounding song rhythm, drags
her cracked feet in the drain, makes room
for unseen children, and amid freight trucks'
brake screams and a fog of diesel fumes,
moaning her desolation, gives imaginary suck.

Making an Impression

I shoulder long grass, my torso
splashed with seeds like coffee grouts.
Near the peak a white whale-back
boulder protrudes. I lie down

panting. Last night's rain has peeled
the blue-gums' bark and their sticky
trunks glisten nude, like mine soaking
into the rock. My half-open eye

captures leaves twirling equally
in the wind with clouds which bulge
and darken, far as the light-blue sky
or near as eyelash moisture.

Four miles below hums the town
where my frail achievements fester.
I open the other eye at nightshade
berries and a pale leaf as it cowers

on the rock, making no more impact
than the star shape of myself
as I rise, etched in sweat, which
within seconds the sun devours.

Safari Slides

A projector's light
beams through
the mango trees
and palpable night.

Our host bawls
above the cicadas:

'From the Rover
we snapped this rhino
at 50 miles per hour.'

A fly crawls,
besotted, on the lens;
its magnified
groping feelers
shudder
across the screen
towards the shadow
of his tense
pedantic neck.

Afro-canned

A work-gang, straddling the beach-bar
roof, their spines a dazzle of sweat-
fractured light, heads wrapped in rags,
meticulously tack and trim layers of straw.
A British thatching expert with raw knees
supervises from the shade of a fig tree.

Motorboats chug their load of bikinis
and floral bermudas back from viewing
cormorants on haze-blurred islands. These
renovations will allow exoticists
authentic afro-gloom to sip highballs
as the sun slants, tip the barman for his
efficient ice cubes, and anticipate
the goat-hide tom-tom's dinner call.

Gaborone

From the *stoep* expats
sip beer, noses
prickling at the *braai*
(stoked placidly by
a chef whose high
hat on black head
matches his teeth's
dapper-gleam).
Honey-limbed girls
bouncing with
belligerent shrieks
venture higher
on wooden walk-
ways which interlock
with tree tops.
Trilling birds hop
on the perimeter
fence, where poinsettia
curls discreetly round
the razor wire.

Floor Show

Brown legs stamp
in triple crash
anklets rattling.

Slim arms point
skywards, eyes roll
glazed and proud.

Lithe bodies squirm,
Ingoma rhythms
urging passion.

Brown legs stamp;
no answering dust
rises from the polished
parquet floor.

Candles flicker
on the shiny faces
of diners, amused,
witty, replete.

One, half-drunk,
applauding, hurls
a coin towards
the dancers; it spins

bounces against
an afro-chic carved
idol and drops
at the waiters' feet.

Embarrassment swells
against the clapping
rhythm. The dancers
fade. They retreat

wriggling defiance.
Hi-fi muzak
plasters over cracks

in the mock-thatched
roof. While wires
are disentangled

the boys behind
screens wipe away
war paint, emerging

sheepish in school
blazers and shorts with
ruler-sharp creases.

Swimming Pool Sacrament

My snorting serpent's
angle sees wind splash
the sky with spray plucked
away towards banana leaves'
ragged flutter, pulsing

like last night's wet-tight
grip of brown and white
limbs – snake-striped spasm –
plunged into crystal depths.

For this death, birth and fluid
life-growth my daytime
body turbine self unscrewing
is Extreme Unction, Baptism
and drum-slashed Passage Rite.

Close Shaves

Our first reconciliation laid the seed:
as the taxi bumper-crawled, a gale-snapped
eucalyptus thwacked with vicious speed
(yet dream-sick slowness) the car ahead;
we fled the rescuing ambulance to trapped
bedroom passions, unexpectedly freed.

Even amid frigid flames of hell-hate,
shared frights (curfews, an exploding TV,
police phone taps, our son's delayed
malarial recovery, or spattered grave dust
on a friend's coffin) could, with compulsive
healing, electrify old lusts.

In middle age, calamities stay in sight;
if love doesn't bind us, then fear might.

Elemental

The man above is supposed to rain
on the woman's cracked, hot earth.

But we have been so long tight-locked
drenching each other with love swirls,
we know neither plenty nor dearth,
up nor down, mortar/pestle, fool/
genius, hot/cold, pleasure/pain,
blue/brown, sun, cloud, hail nor rock,

but one fecund storm-pool
where all the elements whirl.

Haunted

Old houses send ironic shivers through these zebra marriages.
Like that Louisiana hotel – staying in the oak-panelled
'Old Slave Quarters', my insomniac African wife kept
me nightlong switching the kaleidoscope of TV channels.

But this boulder-trussed Zomba mansion, marooned in pines,
echoing with dogs and imperial ghosts, cuts deeper.
Rain torrents prise open the corrugated roof. Wisteria
dislodges crumbling cement. My kaftaned wife inclines
from her perch amid potted *khonde* ferns, dispatching
the gardener to stoke our rust-thin firewood geyser.

Air bubbles drive the water pipes, stuttering like a trapped
metallic turboprop orchestra, and the drains beneath
peeling paint-scabs block themselves monthly, threatening
Armageddons of backward-exploding colonial crap.

A Hard Rain

The bedroom curtain flapped;
thunder rolled; the ground
hissed with rain as if
our shudders conjured other
storms outside.

My after-bath
hair-slicked-down face
glistens as if with knowledge
in the driving mirror.

Roadside earth tangs
waft through the windows
and strings of bark hanging
like streamers cling
to the battered blue-gums.

Programmed

On the third row
in the third booth,
she bends her hot-cross
bun black head.

Concentration
stoops her soft nape.

She pouts and grins
in the air, or sulks
twisting lips round
vowels.

        I tune in.

Tangling wires
(jack plugs plunged
tight in sockets)
connect us.

My corrections
(sweet discipline)
are caresses breathed
through my mike.

Submissive, she smiles
at commendation.

My grave
pedagogue
big brother
face, reflected
from the booth's glass,
superimposes
on her, fiddling
with the earphones.

Examinations

Assuming the bureaucrat's dry
manipulative poise I discharge
question sheets (equations,
theories, translations, data ...)

Parallel lines of black heads
lean into the future beneath
a hum of fluorescent bulbs.

Outside, a lakescape panorama
fades, where *my* ancestors,
amid malarial swamps with gun
and Bible, pacified *theirs*.

Ball-points stab at papers
like assagai.

Sages

Upon reading an African poet

We also have our sages.
Not veteran *Chopa* dancers
proudly stamping their traditions
into the earth. Nor sly
grandmothers crouching over fires,
stringing proverbs like beads
on threads of trickster tales.

But grizzled heads in dank
pubs, soaking toothless gums
in half pints of ale,
babble of war wounds
coronations and mining disasters.
Or shuffling through deserted
streets where wind sweeps
the market refuse, a woman
hunts for cabbage stalks,
and staring stubbornly from
bloodshot eyes, hurls curses
at blackened warehouse walls.

Starlight

The day the poet (after four
years in a windowless cell)
was released I drove him with
exultant chatter to his place
through a night of pale-straw
hills, and saying 'I'd almost
forgotten how stars looked'
he leaned back as if to lick
them from his upturned face
on which torrents of starlight
fell

Southern Cross

You seem to flare just
above a point where
sand and *fynbos* lull
the Indian Ocean.

But here clouds dust
the European sky,
as you feverishly toss
curtains back to cull
a mirage of street
lamps, which cheat
you into searching
for the Southern
Cross.

Tangles

On a Sculpture Exhibition by Berlings Kaunda

We know all about *their* tangles,
the promises which lure into dead forests,
the vine convolutions dangling poisoned fruits,
the arbours which sprout lacerating threats,
the solidities which writhe into fanged despair.

Your tangles glisten with the sanity of sunbeams,
they luxuriate, probe memories, sanctify,
quiver with carnal winds, shoot sap into roots,
entwine and germinate our dreams.

For a moment, while we let the sheen
of these sculptured seeds fructify,
your tangles help us evade *theirs*.

Return of the Linguist

'Malawi's only semanticist' your letter self-scoffed.
Jokes aside, this place, with lost seams of gossip
and taboo-coated rhetoric lodged deep in fissures,
needs your skills – wild pickaxing or delicate
chiselling for fossilised signs.
                                        It needs
the deftest rinsing in gallons of sweat to sieve
a single gem of meaning.

Tongues

The old Xhoa woman's bliss is
to allow her mouth free play
to bunch its stops, trills
and a delicately pursed, labial
click. How can we kill
a tongue in which, all day,
the mouth blows kisses?

Other Languages

There they really do things
differently – cucumber-sliced
slivers of spliced agglutination.
A thousand toxic pixies
stagger through parataxis.
Those antonyms and triple
negatives! Such sleight
of tongue and tweezer-tight
control! Angels dancing
on a velar fricative!

But if, through tip-toe
balance and creeper-clung
grip, you survive that steamy
jungle, the retroflex rains,
piranha plosives, the doom-
clogged rivers of hollow
logs and supersegmental
squids, one day clouds begin
to swirl away, and mountains
of meaning brilliantly loom.

Prayer Rock

Near the highway in what's left of the bush,
a Zionist apostle sways, white-robed against the grass,
her arms raised towards a rock which she touches
with her *doekie*, tenderly, repeatedly and fast.

    *

God of our fathers
help Thabo, my
plump grandson,
though he squeals
and stuffs insects
into his mouth.
        And God help
        Lebogang
        only seventeen,
        still at school,
        with thin legs,
        though she's made
        me a granny.
And God help
the new one I'm
sure Lebo has
started in her
swollen belly,
though he'll need
nappies, juice
and vaseline.
        And God help
        my son-in-law,
        though I don't
        know his name,
        and no doubt
        he'll slink
        off just
        like the last.

And God help my
customers, though
they grumble at
hems or seams
and make false
promises of month-
end payments.
      And God help
      my eyes which
      squint and water,
      though my lamp,
      reeking paraffin,
      illuminates
      fine stitching
      on cushion covers.
And God please
again, especially
help Thabo who'll
soon scamper to
the road where
whores drop
condoms, cars
scream, and drunks
hurl empty cans.

      *

Behind the rock a machine's beak cranks and guillotines
the earth, which puffs back with clanging dread.
A disturbed hoopoe, flying from dust to circle the scene,
descants Mma Lebo's moans as she quivers from toe to head.

Furnace

Firewood crackled
flames roared
in the cracked
grey tight-
packed conical
clay oven.
Japhet with goat-
skin bellows
fanned the flames
and his father,
Suzgo, with
rusty tongs
gripped the rock
praying until
his great-grand-
father's skill
helped guide
the bulbous clod
into the aperture.
Suzgo, eyes
smoke-smarting,
extracted the red-
throbbing ore.
Japhet held
tongs as Suzgo,
to the sizzle
of sprinkled
water, hammered
molten metal
into a hoe.

The Polish
tractor, gleaming
in noon sun,

chugs and hoots
into the village.
Women waving
branches torn
off trees
ululate
their praise.
Japhet hitches
the plough,
grins in proud
driver's pose,
delves the earth
with stone-clanged
ease and turns
five rows
of immaculate
furrows.

The tractor's
paint peels
and fades,
grass grows
deep around
punctured wheels.
Japhet has fled
to a town garage.
The Poles
have migrated
to Europe,
and the village
cannot replace
the shattered
prop-shaft.
Suzgo
with patient
old man's craft
rehabilitates
the furnace.

Unaided he starts
the slow task
of prising
and hacking
from the marooned
machine sharp
shards to melt
in his furnace
and transmute
into new
hoe blades.

Lifestyles

You eat off the finest bone china,
the silence broken by fork scrapes.
We eat from a wooden bowl,
with merriment dripping off fingers.

Your wine, from choicest grapes,
adorns place mats with stains of anger.
Ours, from crushed prickly pear
and mulberries, fuels forgiveness.

Your bodies, gleaming with gold,
slither on silk away from each other.
We lie on a river-reed mattress,
and cries of love fill the air.

Globalisation

Blue eyes outstare the sand-light;
winds fan dune-haunch fire.
An androgynous land sizzles, branded
can-stuffed, stacked tight
in the tortured symmetry of desire.

IMF Consultant

Was it Algiers
or Bucharest
adjusting
the air-con,
maybe Maputo,
Khartoum
or Ho Chi
Minh City,
in mid e-
mail pursuit,
of starved
refugees,
where pity
closed down,
like a snapped
shut lap-top,
and suddenly
I exposed
the bloody
bandaged fears
our latest
fiscal bomb
had carved?

A Ballad for the 'Goodies'

How you loved to play the gunslinger
who won poor peasants' trust
with integrity and a trigger-finger,
sending baddies sprawled in the dust!

I followed you to bilharzia swamps,
an aproned bosom absorbing cares.
I brought vaccines, pills and tilly lamps
to enlighten obscure village squares.

You were the hero whose skill, vigour
and grit would avert a Third World War
with fertiliser, dams and fiscal rigour
following sunsets on your 4x4.

And your efforts did make flourish
cattle ranches and golf greens
but the peasants were only nourished
on booze and weavily beans.

Can't you see there is no rising sun,
our policies smother and divide,
the Third World War has already begun
and we're on the baddies' side?

The Maxi's Last Jaunt

In memory of Eric Kerr

Each summer like migratory birds
we flew from Africa, my brown children
in screeching reunion with my white,
and, snug as gift-wrapped Kendal Mint-
Cake, we squeezed into dad's old Maxi
which he yearly cajoled with Duckhams,
spanners and Turtle Wax into survival
miracles. The rust-corroded floor
pulsed to the stamp of exultant feet,
as the car radio throbbed and hair
streamed by open windows. Dad always
griped about taking him from Coventry
to his Cumbrian birthplace to climb
Skiddaw and watch clouds scudding over
Solway Firth, but there was never room
in the jalopy, crammed with clothes
and blankets as we slept under stars
and terrorised mountains or rivers
with whoops of savage, family laughter,
gulping joys we knew couldn't last.

This year my bearded rock-drummer son
and dreadlocked daughter come with
Dad on the back seat, stopping at his
favourite haunts, Swaledale, Penrith,
Aira Force and Troutbeck. When we
sweat through Dodd Wood and strike
along the edge of Ullock Pike, our
shared backpack is heavy with snacks,
sweaters and Dad's remains in a plastic
Co-op mortuary urn. At the ritual
opening a wind whistles from the Solway

swirling his ashes across a heathery
spur, plush as satin. Our regrets,
but not our lingering guilt, seem
to stream away with the vanishing dust,
before we return in haste to Coventry
where we sell the Maxi for seventy quid
on the exact expiry date of its M.O.T.

Children at Play (Leeds/Harare)

Kids clatter skateboards
pitting curves against
rectangular concrete.

      *

Child-scavengers outwit
crows skimming the park
for crumbs picnickers drop.

Kite

I should have known that kids
who shelter in patched packing-case
hovels, snatching mealie scraps
and unripe bananas, would have the wit
by joining patient strips of plastic
thread to transform those potato
sacks half-buried in garbage,
and hoist the polythene kite against
wind buffets, while dusty legs cascade
in unison, and the kite dips, resisting,
till in slow response to the climax
of tugging it swoops, soars
and glides, tail flapping high above
the mud walls and tin roofs.

Bouquets

In the chill of fern-filled halls,
experts, wrangling for hours,
lob, like squash balls, half-born
budgets across polished tables.

An extrusion
of microchipped
resolutions:
'informal sector
participation ...
utility skill
transfer ...
import
substitution.'

Outside, a ragamuffin uses teeth
and pavement heat to coax torn
ladies' tights and rusty wire
into bouquets of artificial flowers.

Song of the Seed Disposers

We'll never make babies (short
fists clutching our fingers, the clothes-
line proudly flapping nappy flags).
We'll never debate the merits
of boarding schools (bank loans
for termly bills and crumpled reports).
No grandchildren will demand sweets
or sob their nightmares into our laps.

All those sticky futures we drop
into black, plastic bin bags.
But, oh the comforting treats, sighs,
breathless promises, laughter, moans,
slithery flesh and closed eyes
which go into the non-making!

Seed Music

In this country of seeds where shrubs flick
burrs moist-clinging to shirt and ankles
where guavas pomegranates grenadillas squirt
juice on the palate and garrulous crones
warn of excess seeds which, lodged in the belly,
sprout trees thorns and flamboyant fruit;
where village mothers who with regular pestle
splats pulverise nuts and daily maize,
lampoon in panting throaty songs their too
mean, too horny or recalcitrant men,
seed cycle's music offers little relief;
hardships of belly and womb are also percussive.

AIDS Ward

The family whisper, fingering magazines
she'll never read. One chants throatily
to a rattle of rosary beads. Petunias
in a coke bottle vie with urine smells
soaking into rubber.

What flesh left on the skeleton
under stained sheets can extrude
from her face (which pain pulls
tight as a goat-skin drum) those
few lucid drops of sweat?

Her eyes strain from their hollows
as if to pull memories, dancing through
days before wedlock, days of bloom,
teeth glittering on magazine covers,
the same teeth which now protrude
from purple lips flecked with foam.

The eyes flickering from kinfolk,
searching perhaps for her husband,
settle on the delicate sway of flowers
and suddenly dilate, as if in frozen
screams of accusation.

Bare Truths

Here, where even village herbalists assemble
in jackets and ties, where tuxedoed demagogues
patch dreams with garish java-print wraps,
where the mouths of worshippers are gagged
by starched swirling vestments, where the sick
and starving bury each other in shrouds
embroidered with developmental slogans,
where policemen polish nonconformist skulls
to a meticulous button-bright patina,
that mad girl, sprinting stark naked, knew
what she was doing, clothes tied on a stick
brandished at pedestrians, terrifying cars
with feral eyes, before shimmering through
bushes like a duiker into the forest depths.

The Continuing Search

At independence she proudly named her son
'Uhuru',
not knowing that, one distraught day, years
later,
searching the urine-dank maze of shanty-town
alleys
she would be arrested for telling a secret
cop,
with guileless truth, she was looking for
'Uhuru'.

Sunday Exercise

Each Sunday Apostolic women clap
and dance on boulders after all-night hymns.
Today I jog past rock pools, mud-trapped
beer cans and dumps of rusty air-vents;
I percolate, through wind and loosened limbs,
a week of rain and phoned endearments
to my sick mother two continents away.
The women, stripped to the waist
or with hitched-up robes, still pray,
bathing sweaty thigh, shoulder or breast
in some, I suppose, spring equinox
ancient cleansing or neo-baptismal rite.
They laugh at my embarrassment in flight
to quiet scrubland where a matted layer
of grass and earth, beneath flocks
of weaver birds, sprouts aromatic ferns
as rain falls on my face, turned
upward in its own crooked lustral prayer.

A Mother's Last Song

In memory of Anne Kerr

When I raise
my head to death
as once to your
first cry
it's not *my* eyes
which turn to stone
but *yours* gazing
with ignorant
pity at me
slowly burning
into melody.

Working Women

1. The Translator

TV lamps catch the mogul's glasses
as he stoops to smooth an errant
lapel. His guttural syllables fade
and your voice, soothing over like
an aural spreadsheet, starts to list
cost benefits.
                    Hardly visible
behind his shoulder, your powdered
face, glazed with concentration,
makes us wonder if your eyes know
how to blaze or if those articulate
lips ever round to a kiss.

2. Video Editor

She knows the politician so
intimately that after scores
of eloquent, perfectly timed
hands-on-heart and raised fingers
she can roll the whole breath-
flow forwards and back repeatedly
slow and fast till it's refined
to clusters of grunts, hesitations
or squeals, and she can identify
the precise microsecond the lie
begins.

3. Computer Operator

She scrolls with lightning ease
through a shimmer of icons.
Digits, meaningless as sand,
reel in pixilated columns.

Her fingers twitter like
lovebirds across the keys,
and powerful men begin
to tremble in distant lands.

After Chikumbi: Blood Donation

I dashed to the Blood Bank
on a wave of hot-flushed
anger, desperate to offer
my pittance of reparation.
Stuck in a hospital donor queue,
righteous fervour melting
to melancholy, I link-picked
a chain of guilt – the refugees'
limb-tatters to the racist
grenades to the bomb factories
of Europe where workers
drive to cheery pubs (*Daily
Mirror* and warmed-up pies)
a jokey malt-dense culture
I reluctantly recognise as mine.
The blood at last demanded
glugs slowly, enfeebled
by malaria and alcohol,
into an impromptu Sunquick
bottle. In my sweaty langour, I
want the whole body load to seep
through the expiating needle.
A nurse's starched efficiency
bustles me off the bed.
I sip Coca Cola; cotton wool
tucked in my arm crook,
the fist (momentarily
cleansed of irony) is
still half-clenched, as if
in fraternal solidarity.

Tisa's War

On Tuesday the rebels quaffed Tisa's millet brew
grabbed the logs she'd headloaded from the mountain
and roasted her last twine-thin chicken.

On Thursday the loyalists trampled her maize,
spilled water she'd sweat-garnered in earth pots
and left turds steaming across her spinach patch.

On Friday (whether by rebels or loyalists she never knew)
Tisa's daughter was splayed open like a pig carcass
and torn to insanity by a platoon of despots.

On Sunday a land mine found Tisa short-cutting
from church, scattered her charred Bible pages, cassava
and splintered logs, like kindle-twigs in a whirlwind.

Freedom Percussion

During the insurrection, dustbin lids (shields
against rubber bullets) were banged every hour
to taunt cops, and, finally, at a victory parade,
they syncopated the people's ululatory triumph.

The struggle leaders pat wallets which yield
crisp notes, now displaying the new hero's
wise smile, and over cellphones explain
why they cruise behind tinted windows of power.

In the townships, rent-baron thugs intimidate
tenants; potholes loom wider, and women still lug
rusty tin-loads of water from stagnant pools.
At night the dustbin lids begin to clatter again.

The Cross Examination of Sofia Nkosana

The young girls who shyly bring
us water and spiced chicken wings
cast shadows flickering from an oil
lamp against Bible mottoes on the wall.

Their mother shifts in the sofa as if seeking
a piece of village gossip to elaborate.

Her quiet words spit at my face.

Hurled naked and hungry into a bare cell,
kicked till she cleared the stale shit
off the floor, the long night chill
fractured by spasms of electric shocks.
'Give me water.' 'Bitch drink your piss!'

I scribble notes, weigh the calculus of pain
and arrange the chicken bones on my plastic plate.

The Inspector General's buttons heave with fury.
'Fetch your rebel daughter back or we'll pick
your other children and deal with you again.'

I squirm, mumble advice, dab her wounds with pity.

The girls clear up my mess of bones
and from the kitchen mutely stare.

Later, though impulsive tears evaporate
into faxes, phones to lawyers, Amnesty
International and embassies, why do I wake
at night in a pool of sweat, with the electric
gizmo in my hand, pointing at her bare
flinching shoulders and the garlic
chicken lingering in my throat?

Uprooted

Our hut was an easy walk from my
husband's grave; a path from the sorghum
plot cut past a baobab into the thicket
and I came each month to pour beer and seek
blessings; when the troubles grew worse
and salt was scarce and *banditos* demanded
goats I'd walk deeper into the wood where
the frogs were too frightened to croak,
and I scattered flour on my father's grave,
or deeper still where the creepers twisted
on grandfather's grave, where even grass-
hoppers were silent and the only sound
I could hear was the beat of my heart,
till blessings oozed from the ground,
and calmed me. But the *banditos* came
more often, snatching men or girls;
they burned the school and beat those
too weak to stifle screams. All night
I spat out teeth and blood. I had to flee
with a bundle of clothes, spoons and plastic
cups on my head; Selina, wrapped tight
in calico, drummed her heels against my back;
gunfire boomed like funeral drums, smoke
stung our eyes – no time for last prayers
at the graves of men who'd left me. We
walked past forests, rivers, windswept
mountains till we reached the border
in the gloomy highlands. I kindled
corncobs for warmth, cradling Selina
in my calico. People here showed us hills
for building our shacks of grass
and spattered mud. Some men dug
shallow latrines near our huts
which huddled by the rocks for shelter.

Once a week, smiling uniformed white
women came in landrovers to give us
each a basket of flour, beans and medicine
for coughs; when I stagger to the stream
with my water pot, suckling Selina, tears
flow not for the scabies on our skin,
or the hard mat where we shiver all night,
but because I never had time to pour
my last flour and beer on the graves
in our home thicket, and all of us have
left parents' graves in many villages.
Preachers roar all night in the camp
about Armageddon and the horned beast,
saying that even here people quarrel,
and some have fled across distant borders.
The priests (who claim to know) say Satan
is uprooting the whole world, and spirits
are howling around neglected graves like
these cold winds through stunted grass.

Our Year of Living Dangerously

Strange how in this insurrection, where courage insists
on sprouting unexpectedly – smuggled samizdat pamphlets,
anti-government slogans scattered at dawn, whispered
assignations behind trees with rebels, furtively faxed
briefings, defiance of police threats (those late-night
interrogations, rumours of deportation, hit lists
and detentions, the loosened wheel-nuts or multi-holed
mysterious punctures) – eros also throbs, each frenetic
perhaps-the-last embrace shuddering into a mutual rite
of solidarity, secret blessings liberally bestowed.

Safe as Houses

A house built on a sun-baked plain
is without the fine element of danger.
Naturally, swirls of sand grains
settle on curtains, books and window
shelves; or precariously shallow lines
of brick footings send cracks
zig-zag up the walls. But it lacks
that exquisite doom of the steep
forest where a mountain monster
once, to thunderclap applause,
lashed its tail, scattering rocks
down the valley, to smash match-box
huts and trees, and even now,
outside the kitchen, below the pines,
a dinosaur boulder lurks, its back
a grey glisten of rain, with claws
sharp, prepared, in one lightning leap,
to attack.

High Density Housing Scheme

I jogged through the arid scrub
only on Sunday mornings, so I
never noticed surveyors erect their
schematic rigging of poles and twine.

A few Sundays later, I saw
(nursing a menopausal paunch)
bulldozers had scraped away shrubs
to leave a grid of ochre roads.

Lurking beneath trees and dangled
nests, tar-spreaders, ready to launch
excretions of macadam and road signs,
began to shimmer in dawn fires.

Unseen workers filled each trench
with hard core and a neat brick-course.
One Sunday identical patterns of angled
plastic conduits had been imposed.

The next, six-metre-square
concrete slabs stretched in rows
to the horizon. Erect snake wires
flashed junction-box mirror-heads.

On the furthest slab a wind glides
dust swirling to my parched mouth,
and dead leaves whirl like ghosts
greedy to possess these future lives.

Midair Encounter

As the plane began to list
he, a builder, bawdy
expert on gutters, roof
struts and bituminous felt,
met me, dramaturg, dream
mechanic, fumbler of masks,
screams and painted lies.

He proudly pointed, as we
lost height, to the proof
of his creation, gaudy
tiles, solid and sun-kissed.
The splayed townscape melted
mine to mirage, the gleam
in scattered strangers' eyes.

Other People's Houses

Roaming worker, I spill
my life unpacking and packing,
fixing fuses or handles, rawl-
plugging walls to hang
my pictures, mowing lawns
seeded by distant owners,
and wondering if pot plants
that wilt and jostle in vans
from home to home will
ever find peace to flower.

A Tongue's Biography

The poet's chill trickle
of Scots, spilled pure
as malt over ice,
makes me despise
my own mud vowels –
the glottal Cumbrian
scoured with Fylde sand
and Brum slate, sullied
with Geordie claats,
all blanched bland
with sun steaming through
Malawian creepers, and my
cracked syllables mourn
such hybrid ooze
seeping into the globe's
remotest gullies.

Notes

p.12   *biltong*: Afrikaans word for meat dried in the sun.

p.17   *stoep*: Afrikaans for veranda.
braai: Afrikaans for barbecue

p.18   *Ingoma*: a war dance of the Ngoni people.

p.23   *khonde*: chiChewa for veranda.

p.27   *Chopa*: a popular village dance in Northern Mozambique and Southern Malawi.

p.28   *fynbos*: scrub vegetation found in dry areas of South Africa.

p.30   Xhoa is the name of a group of San (bushmen) from Central Botswana, who live on the fringes of the Kalahari Desert. It is also the name of their language. There are about 2000 mostly elderly Xhoa speakers. Within two or three decades the language will probably be extinct.

p.32   *doekie*: Afrikaans for headscarf.

p.47   *Uhuru*: kiSwahili for 'freedom', a common slogan during the 1960s in East Africa, and occasionally used as a name.

p.52   Chikumbi was a refugee camp belonging to the Zimbabwean African People's Union, outside Lusaka in Zambia. On 19 October 1978 Rhodesian air-borne forces bombed the camp, causing many casualties.